PISCES

PiSCES
20 February–20 March

PATTY GREENALL & CAT jAVOR

MQP

Published by MQ Publications Limited
12 The Ivories
6–8 Northampton Street
London N1 2HY
Tel: 020 7359 2244
Fax: 020 7359 1616
Email: mail@mqpublications.com
Website: www.mqpublications.com

Copyright © MQ Publications Limited 2004
Text copyright © Patty Greenall & Cat Javor 2004

Illustrations: Gerry Baptist

ISBN: 1-84072-664-4

1 3 5 7 9 0 8 6 4 2

Printed in Italy

INTRODUCTION

WHAT IS **ASTROLOGY?**

Astrology is the practice of interpreting the positions and movements of celestial bodies with regard to what they can tell us about life on Earth. In particular it is the study of the cycles of the Sun, Moon, and the planets of our solar system, and their journeys through the twelve signs of the zodiac— Aries, Taurus, Gemini, Cancer, Leo, Virgo, Libra, Scorpio, Sagittarius, Capricorn, Aquarius, and Pisces—all of which provide astrologers with a rich diversity of symbolic information and meaning.

Astrology has been labeled a science, an occult magical practice, a religion, and an art, yet it cannot be confined by any one of these descriptions. Perhaps the best way to describe it is as an evolving tradition.

Throughout the world, for as far back as history can inform us, people have been looking up at the skies and attaching stories and meanings to what they see there. Neolithic peoples in Europe built huge stone structures such as Stonehenge in southern England in order to plot the cycles of the Sun and Moon, cycles that were so important to a fledgling agricultural society. There are star-lore traditions in the ancient cultures of India, China, South America, and Africa, and among the indigenous people of Australia. The ancient Egyptians plotted the rising of the star Sirius, which marked the annual flooding of the Nile, and in ancient Babylon, astronomer-priests would perform astral divination in the service of their king and country.

Since its early beginnings, astrology has grown, changed, and diversified into a huge body of knowledge that has been added to by many learned men and women throughout history. It has continued to evolve and become richer and more informative, despite periods when it went out of favor because of religious, scientific, and political beliefs.

Offering us a deeper knowledge of ourselves, a profound insight into what motivates, inspires, and, in some cases, hinders, our ability to be truly our authentic selves, astrology equips us better to make the choices and decisions that confront us daily. It is a wonderful tool, which can be applied to daily life and our understanding of the world around us.

The horoscope—or birth chart—is the primary tool of the astrologer and the position of the Sun, Moon, Mercury, Venus, Mars, Jupiter, Saturn,

Uranus, Neptune, and Pluto at the moment a person was born are all considered when one is drawn up. Each planet has its own domain, affinities, and energetic signature, and the aspects or relationships they form to each other when plotted on the horoscope reveal a fascinating array of information. The birth, or Sun, sign is the sign of the zodiac that the Sun was passing through at the time of birth. The energetic signature of the Sun is concerned with a person's sense of uniqueness and self-esteem. To be a vital and creative individual is a fundamental need, and a person's Sun sign represents how that need most happily manifests in that person. This is one of the most important factors taken into account by astrologers. Each of the twelve Sun signs has a myriad of ways in which it can express its core meaning. The more a person learns about their individual Sun sign, the more they can express their own unique identity.

ZODIAC WHEEL

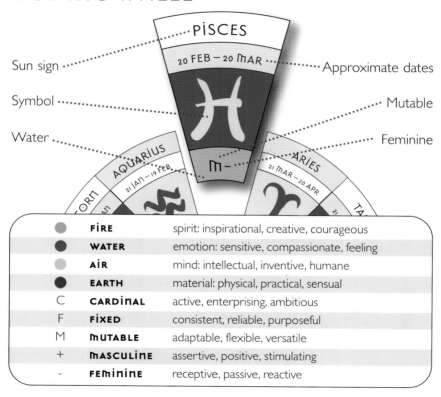

Sun sign

Symbol

Water

Approximate dates

Mutable

Feminine

PISCES

20 FEB – 20 MAR

AQUARIUS   21 JAN – 19 FEB

ARIES   21 MAR – 20 APR

●	**FIRE**	spirit: inspirational, creative, courageous
●	**WATER**	emotion: sensitive, compassionate, feeling
●	**AIR**	mind: intellectual, inventive, humane
●	**EARTH**	material: physical, practical, sensual
C	**CARDINAL**	active, enterprising, ambitious
F	**FIXED**	consistent, reliable, purposeful
M	**MUTABLE**	adaptable, flexible, versatile
+	**MASCULINE**	assertive, positive, stimulating
-	**FEMININE**	receptive, passive, reactive

PART ONE

THE **ESSENTIAL** PISCES

RULERSHİPS

Pisces is the twelfth and final sign of the zodiac. It is traditionally ruled by the planet Jupiter but Neptune also has an affinity with it. The symbol for Pisces is the Fishes—two of them swimming in opposite directions and joined by a golden cord. There are earthly correspondences of everything in life for each of the Sun signs. The part of the human body that Pisces represents is the feet. Pisces is a Mutable and Feminine sign. Gemstones for Pisces are aquamarine, cat's eye, amethyst, and jade. Pisces also signifies rivers full of fish, ponds, wells, fountains, water lilies, aquariums, and fish themselves. It is also associated with dancers, poets, escape artists, spiritualists, drugs, and alcohol as well as convents, hospitals, institutions, cinema, film, photography, and the imagination.

PISCES

The part of the human body that Pisces represents is the feet.

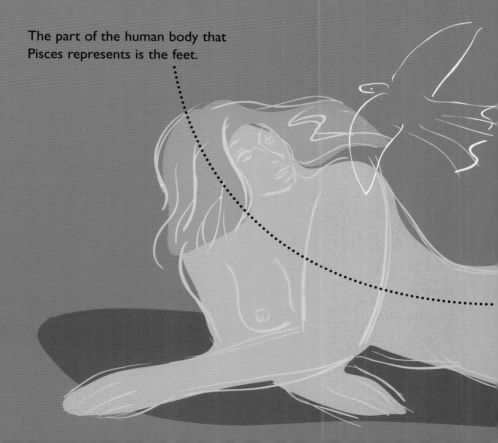

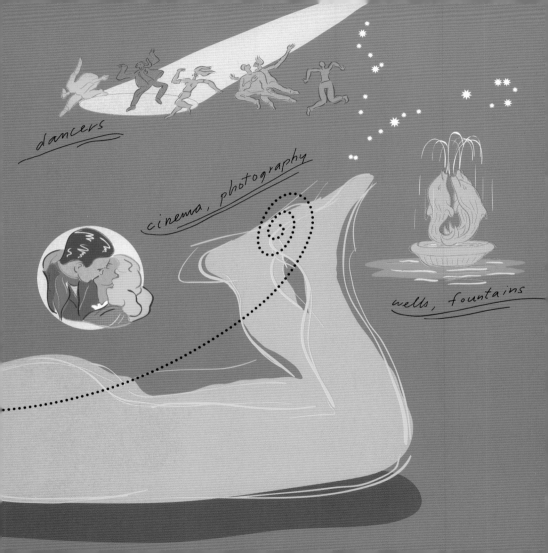

dancers

cinema, photography

wells, fountains

PERSOПALITY

"Empathetic," "gentle," and "kind" are words that are commonly used to describe Pisces, yet these individuals have so many sides to them that they actually defy description. It would almost be easier to look in a dictionary of adjectives and just list all of them. Having been born under the last sign of the zodiac, Pisceans are thought to have gathered something from each of the preceding Sun signs, which is why they are so good at putting themselves in other people's shoes. They feel deeply for others, but their sympathy doesn't stop there; they would probably give their last cent to someone who seemed to be suffering more than they were. This means that they have a strong charitable streak, which is why they often end up as the victim, but when they do, they know, at some level, that they have chosen that role.

This leads us to the sacrificial theme that runs through Pisces. A Pisces can be something of a martyr, but things are rarely as simple as that, for Pisces is just as capable as anyone of having an agenda, bearing a grudge, or being angry; the difference is that it's just not as visible. They're inscrutable, and while it's true that they're gentle and kind, yet there are so many other truths about them. Like the Fishes, they are iridescent, multicolored, ever-changing, and completely impossible to pin down. The symbol of the Fishes swimming in opposite directions but tied together by a thread—the thread of consciousness—encapsulates perfectly the vision these enigmatic people have; no matter which way they approach life they feel that everything is ultimately connected and what appears to have meaning also appears to be totally meaningless. It's as though Pisceans are in this world, but aren't truly part of it.

Largely due to their ability to visualize almost any set of circumstances, Pisceans are also versatile and adaptable. There are simply no words to describe the breadth of the Pisces imagination; it's as vast as the universe and as difficult to comprehend, even for Pisceans themselves, and it works in a number of splendidly different ways, most of which are positive—but not all. Pisceans can meld into new situations like magic and if necessary, can even seem to disappear completely. This adaptability is useful when it comes to dealing with life's inevitable disappointments. They'll just shrug their shoulders and carry on. Even when they're slighted by others, they're usually able to let the slight roll off them like water off a duck's back! Or if they're faced with some insult or injury, something inside them simply lets go so that they're able to drift away from the hurt without putting up any resistance. It's their best form of self-protection.

They'll bounce back quickly, but experience doesn't stop them from being too trusting or from making the same mistakes time after time. They have a memory span akin to that of a goldfish—a matter of seconds! It must be remembered, however, that Pisceans have sensitive, vulnerable souls, so anyone dealing with them needs to treat them with the utmost gentleness. And although they themselves can be brash at times, they have an aversion to anything harsh and they definitely respond best to thoughtful tenderness and soothing, relaxing environments.

Being of the element of Water, Pisces is also known as a fertile, creative sign, which accounts for its natives' musical, poetic, and artistic skills. And it's in the world of artistic endeavor that Pisces' profound vision serves its most divine purpose. Pisceans have a heaven-sent ability to leave their body, figuratively speaking, float away, and return with some ethereal piece of inspiration that would not be understood by mere mortals were it not for Pisces' ability to convey it in artistic terms. Indeed, if there is one thing that can really attach Pisceans to reality, then it's the dedication they show to producing works of great beauty and insight. Yet Pisceans are more than simply insightful; they're also highly intuitive, some would say psychic. They absorb the vibes around them like a sponge, which can be difficult for other people to deal with.

Sometimes referred to as deceptive, Pisceans don't intend to pull the wool over anyone's eyes but what they might do is deceive themselves into believing a different version of the truth, for they're capable of discovering brand-new facets of reality in their already scintillating world, or of creating a new reality in their minds in the blink of an eye. So if they were asked "What is the truth?" they wouldn't be able to come up with an answer that totally satisfies on every level—and they can access more levels than anybody else! Thanks to their bountiful imaginations, their only reply could be "Everything and nothing is the truth."

Pisceans will find it intolerable if they feel they're being limited by anything, particularly by someone else's perception of them, so they will often cloud issues to avoid being pigeonholed. And they'll avoid pigeonholing others in return, rarely ever sitting in judgment on people's behavior or ideas, even though they might not necessarily agree with them. They see the infinite capacity of every human being to express all aspects of humanity and they accept that everyone is part of nature's vast variety.

Pisces is a very idealistic, romantic, and spiritual sign. Its natives open their hearts and their senses, and steer their way through life in the hope of feeling connected on some level to everyone and everything. Having such empathy and compassion toward others means that they can be very sentimental and frequently tearful because of the immensity of the emotions that others feel—from joy and happiness to sorrow and anger. They grieve with those that feel loss and laugh with those that are glad. Romantic relationships are one way Pisceans have of exploring the possibilities of merging with another soul, so they are often in love with the idea of love as much as with the other person. Pisceans are indescribable people, mysterious, enigmatic, full of riddles, and with a transcendent quality— though it may also be said that they possess every quality.

CAREER & MONEY

Pisces is a caring, responsible, and earnest worker—at least, in short bursts! Pisceans have some admirable qualities but staying power isn't one of them, unless they happen to be working for a cause they believe in and in a field they really love, in which case they can totally immerse themselves. It's true that they can put up with difficult work situations or will stick to a job they don't like in order to pay the bills or because they feel beholden, but they are rarely conventional in the workplace. It's not like them to be predictable and hand in their notice, then work it out. At best, they'll hand in their notice, then simply vanish, but what's more likely is that one day they'll simply decide that they've had enough and will do a disappearing act. Then they'll celebrate by going on a shopping spree or out to a lavish lunch. They'll never look back and probably won't even bother asking for their final paycheck because, in the greater scheme of things, such details don't really matter to them.

When it comes to money, Pisces is not the most practical of signs but, despite the odds, many Pisceans still manage to amass a fortune. Although Pisces is a "feelings" sign, involved in the realm of spirit and emotions, Pisceans are wise enough not to become emotionally attached to the material world. Perhaps that's why the money just seems to roll in as fast as they spend it. There are dry spells, of course, but on the whole, Pisceans have an inner belief that everything will be okay. It usually is, and sometimes it's even better than they imagined.

When Pisceans find themselves in a career of their own choosing, or one that they instinctively know is their calling, they'll sacrifice every last ounce of their energy to it, and may even pour their own resources into it if it's something they really believe in. Then they don't find work unpleasant but instead thrive on it, for it gives their life meaning. Belief in what they're doing is key; all Pisceans need an occupation that's in tune with their beliefs, whether it's selling organic produce, looking after dogs in a dog shelter, or working as a top executive in a multi-million-dollar company. Pisceans are often to be found in jobs where they can give something of themselves, for example healing professions, the clergy, as a mystic, or a medium. With their sense of devotion to a cause, many are employed as veterinarians, anesthetists, doctors, or nurses. They also possess a strong sense of justice; the legal world offers them a place where they can fight for the underdog. But it's in the arts, where the imaginary and real worlds meet, that most Pisceans excel, as photographers, movie directors, musicians, actors, and artists. This is the essence of Pisces.

THE PİSCES **CHİLD**

The need for peace, tranquility, and security is apparent in the Pisces child from the moment he or she comes into the world, though the parents of one of these sweet little children may not enjoy much peace and tranquility themselves in the very early weeks after the birth. However, Pisces children's noisy protests at leaving the safety of the womb and confronting the real world will be short-lived once they get used to and inspired by the new sensations and possibilities around them.

There's an innate joy and innocence in Pisces children that often brings out the protective instincts of people who wish to shield them from the world, and as they are so sensitive to every subtle nuance and vibration in the emotional atmosphere, their behavior often reflects the feelings of those around them. They're rather shy children, who really benefit from a calm, soothing environment and who require a lot of encouragement in order to grow in self-confidence. They may initially resist the strange experience of going off to school, but once they become comfortable with the routine, they're usually popular with classmates and teachers alike. Their wonderful imaginations often begin to reveal themselves in their inclination toward the more creative subjects such as art, music, creative writing, and games. They may at times be caught gazing out of the window, their minds lost in a daydream, but they're usually very sound, all-round students, who are good at absorbing information and knowledge in lesson time.

As they grow into adolescence, their need to retreat into their own inner world becomes more apparent. Teenage Pisceans will frequently be found lying around their bedroom listening to music, writing poetry, or simply gazing into space. They may need a little bit of gentle persuasion to socialize, but trying to bully them into being more outgoing will only have the opposite effect. Young Pisceans are tender, loving, sensitive souls, and when they're content, they can have an almost healing effect on those around them.

PERFECT **GIFTS**

It's really not hard to choose a gift for Pisces. These individuals like pretty much everything and anything! And if they see that even the smallest amount of thought has gone into the choice of gift, they'll be so touched that they'll get all misty-eyed just thinking about that, never mind about the gift itself! But Pisceans are most easily hurt by a lack of thought; for them, something is always better than nothing. To really please a Pisces, the perfect gift is something shiny and multicolored that reflects the light or makes an ethereal sound. A prism, a fiber-optic light, or a mobile with tuned metal tubes hanging from it are all possibilities. These gifts create atmosphere and inspire their dreams and imaginations. They always appreciate music and DVDs, and they love gifts of food, drink, and flowers. Jewelry, accessories, or foreign knickknacks that help create a world of make-believe are very welcome, too, while gifts with a mystical twist, such as crystals, incense, candles, or books on the occult, are sure to delight them.

Pisces is perhaps the one sign that won't be offended by a gift of socks or slippers. Pisces rules the feet so socks and slippers are both essential and thoughtful, but make them special in some way—colorful, beaded or sequined, or decorated with a picture of their favorite film character.

FAVORITE **FOODS**

Pisceans have wide-ranging and refined tastes, so they enjoy many different types of cuisine, especially if the food's washed down with a fine wine. They're willing to try anything once and are enthusiastic about international delicacies. One thing is sure, though, if they're out in a restaurant or at someone's home, and they don't get served a dish that really appeals to their taste buds, then they'll only pick at it. If, however, they taste something totally delicious and sensational, they'll clean their plates very thoroughly and will ask for second and, possibly even, third helpings. It's not that Pisceans are gluttonous, only that enough of a good thing is never enough for them. However, as with all the Water signs, Pisceans may have to watch their alcohol consumption; they easily find that the relaxed dreamy glow they get from the "one too many" can be very addictive.

If Pisceans eat the same foods on a too-regular basis, they become bored, so they're usually to be found eating a varied diet, containing all the foods that are needed for good nutrition. They are also particularly fond of exotic desserts flavored with sweet liquors.

FASHION & **STYLE**

Pisceans have a relaxed attitude to the clothes they wear and are easily influenced by others whose look they admire. They rarely ever spend time poring over glossy fashion magazines, and when they're shopping for clothes, they seem almost in a dream, as though they're waiting for inspiration to strike. Unless they're strict in limiting their wardrobe, they're bound to have a very diverse and varied collection of clothing in their closets.

Whether they're wearing smart, formal clothes, or frayed old favorites that they can't bear to throw away, the Pisces fashion plate never looks either exactly in or out of style. Pisceans prefer to dress to suit their mood rather than concern themselves over whether something really suits their body shape, but somehow they usually get it right.

One item that particularly interests Pisceans is their shoes; look in their closet and you're sure to find a stunning collection. They know instinctively that a good pair of shoes can make a cheap outfit look expensive, while a bargain pair of shoes can make an expensive outfit look cheap.

When it comes to colors, they look lovely in soft lavenders, lilacs, and pastel shades of sea-blue and green. They also look good in floppy frills and fringes, and in flowing fabrics with gentle, romantic patterns. If they wear clothes that are too severe, sharp, or angular, the impression will be of the clothes wearing the Pisces rather than the Pisces wearing the clothes.

iDEAL **HOMES**

Pisceans would prefer to reside near their cherished element, water—by the sea, on a lakeshore, or next to a flowing river. If that's not possible, a fountain in the garden or a miniature water feature in the entryway would give them a familiar, homey feeling.

"Eclectic" might best describe a Pisces home. Some Fish have a better sense of style and color-matching than others, but the one theme that runs through all Pisces homes is that of a miscellany of ornaments and objects that Pisces refuses to throw away and that are special to that Pisces. Their homes can take on just about any look, but dotted around the place there will always be objects that have sentimental value. The Pisces home is also ever-changing. Pisceans frequently rearrange, repaint, and redesign in order to reflect their changing moods and their constantly evolving spirit.

Pisces is very good at creating atmosphere in the home. Many Pisceans like to use the colors of the sea—calming hues of blues, greens, and lavenders—to build a magical, fairytale mood that helps them to escape into their world of fantasy.

PART TWO
RISING SIGNS

WHAT IS A **RISING** SIGN?

Your rising sign is the zodiacal sign that could be seen rising on the eastern horizon at the time and place of your birth. Each sign takes about two and a half hours to rise — approximately one degree every four minutes. Because it is so fast moving, the rising sign represents a very personal part of the horoscope, so even if two people were born on the same day and year as one another, their different rising signs will make them very different people.

It is easier to understand the rising sign when the entire birth chart is seen as a circular map of the heavens. Imagine the rising sign — or ascendant — at the eastern point of the circle. Opposite is where the Sun sets — the descendant. The top of the chart is the part of the sky that is above, where the Sun reaches at midday, and the bottom of the chart is below, where the Sun would be at midnight. These four points divide the circle, or birth chart, into four. Those quadrants are then each divided into three, making a total of twelve, known as houses, each of which represents a certain aspect of life. Your rising sign corresponds to the first house and establishes which sign of the zodiac occupied each of the other eleven houses when you were born.

All of which makes people astrologically different from one another; not all Pisceans are alike! The rising sign generally indicates what a person looks like. For instance, people with Leo, the sign of kings, rising, probably walk with a noble air and find that people often treat them like royalty. Those that have Pisces rising frequently have soft and sensitive looks and they might find that people are forever pouring their hearts out to them.

The rising sign is a very important part of the entire birth chart and should be considered in combination with the Sun sign and all the other planets!

THE **RiSiNG SiGNS** FOR PiSCES

To work out your rising sign, you need to know your exact time of birth—if hospital records aren't available, try asking your family and friends. Now turn to the charts on pages 38–43. There are three charts, covering New York, Sydney, and London, all set to Greenwich Mean Time. Choose the correct chart for your place of birth and, if necessary, add or subtract the number of hours difference from GMT (for example, Sydney is approximately ten hours ahead, so you need to subtract ten hours from your time of birth). Then use a ruler to carefully find the point where your GMT time of birth meets your date of birth—this point indicates your rising sign.

PiSCES WiTH **ARiES** RiSiNG

These Pisceans are among the more dynamic ones, because with Aries rising they appear to have an open and up-front manner about them. They move through life with a single-minded "get-what-you-can-out-of-it" attitude. They take action based on instinct and intuition, and these qualities know no limits nor accept any boundaries. They have the daring of youth and an innate trust that, with their ability to take giant leaps of faith, they're capable of amazing feats. However, appearances can be deceptive and despite their dynamism, they are still deeply immersed in a dreamy realm of spiritual longing. Ambition is a means to an end, but with these complex individuals, it's rarely ever the end that others may think they're seeking. Money tends to come easily to them, not only because they have such a laid-back attitude toward the material world, but because they appear blessed—though some might want to call it the luck of the devil!

PISCES WITH **TAURUS** RISING

When Taurus is rising, Pisces is calm, collected, gentle, and kind. These Pisceans appear to have a stability and a solid strength about them. They may be swimming in an ever-changing sea of emotion and imagination, but to others they are sweet, soft, and very grounded. As they mature and grow, they truly become the focused, capable individuals that they hope to be. With their steadiness and devotion, they develop not just strong values, but also the desire for something to aspire to. They have high hopes and usually attain their wishes through hard work and dedication to a cause. They enjoy the company of other people and are infinitely curious about other people's comings and goings. It's no wonder that they usually become deeply trusted and valued friends on whom others will occasionally dump their problems or to whom they'll go for advice, encouragement, and support.

And people will do so because, not only can these Pisceans offer sympathy and serenity for the weary soul, but, since they're also great lovers of luxury, they'll do it in style and comfort, too. There's plenty of love and kindness in this individual's big heart for all who are near and dear.

PISCES WITH **GEMINI** RISING

One of the most impressive talents of the Pisces with Gemini rising is being master of verbalizing the mystical, the complex, and the elusive—things that simple minds have trouble even contemplating. And yet these Pisceans are almost completely unaware of how much they are admired and respected for it. They are lively, chatty, highly amusing people, who have a wonderful sense of fun and who find it almost impossible to take the absurdities of life too seriously—and that includes themselves, for they probably find themselves more absurd than anything. They are so easily bored by the mundane reality of everyday life that they often feel the need to shake things up a bit, go in search of the exciting, and climb to ever-higher levels of experience. It would be easy to believe that this Pisces is just out to enjoy the pleasures of life, flitting from one interest to another and never staying long enough to get much more than a superficial view before they're off again to indulge their insatiable curiosity. But appearances deceive! These Pisceans have the same depth and breadth as the average Pisces, but they spend more time skimming the surface of life in order to acquire an even greater span of intellect and understanding.

PISCES WITH **CANCER** RISING

♋ Pisceans born with Cancer rising are so empathetic, so sensitive, and so emotionally impressionable that they probably look as if they're always on the verge of tears. A quiet and contemplative but strong demeanor is what marks this vastly mystical, spiritual Sun combination, coupled with a high level of intuition and a desire to nurture and protect. It wouldn't be odd to find these gurulike Pisceans sitting on a cliff top overlooking the sea and meditating, surrounded by a crowd of people hungrily awaiting their sage advice and loving words. Yet most of them will probably lead very quiet, traditional lives, building up a good standard of living, doing some traveling, and collecting valuable artifacts from all the wild and wonderful places they visit. Yet home is where their heart is; they need a base to return to once they've come back from their many journeys, both of the mind and the body. Family values are deeply rooted in them and they have a strong need to belong and to feel at one with loved ones. They are caring and sharing with close friends and family, love children, and have a natural ability to teach that is colored by warm affection and interest.

PISCES WITH **LEO** RISING

♌ This is a real glamour puss, but it isn't a false glamour; that of the Pisces born with Leo rising is embedded deep within their character. These Pisceans love the glitter of the high life, sensual, sumptuous surroundings, and the chance to show off to an often devoted, adoring audience. These are happy, smiling people but they have a ferocious pride and a need to be in control. They may also seem a little mysterious, elusive, or secretive because they are highly sensitive to the powerfully moving undercurrents of the unpredictable outside world, and because they feel a need to shield and protect the more vulnerable aspects of their nature. With their penchant for drama and exaggerated expression, the world of film and music often plays a part in their lives, either directly or through some partnership. They're capable of making something out of nothing, and when they're not making a beautiful song and dance, what they're making sometimes ends up as a mountain when a molehill would have sufficed! Generous and warm-hearted, these Pisceans love to have guests and make them feel at home, yet they won't hesitate to say that they want to be alone when they've had enough of being the entertainer.

PISCES WITH **VIRGO** RISING

♍ On the outside, these Pisceans are all cool efficiency and practical organization, but look inside and it would be hard to find a more dreamily romantic or sensually alluring creature than the Pisces with Virgo rising. They may seem a little aloof, detached, or distracted, and it's true that their clever minds can get totally engrossed as they wander through wonderfully complex realms of thought and imagination, but attract their attention and they'll lose interest in anything other than offering themselves completely to the service of others. It's as though they have no ego and care little for their own personal concerns, which is often why others feel they can take advantage of these charming, loving, totally selfless, and giving people. Since they are shy and demure, it takes time for these Pisceans to feel at ease among new faces, yet once they open up, they are attentive and understanding. They listen intently, taking in every aspect of their surroundings as well as what is being said. They have a sharp perception of their environment and, although they might appear to be unknowing, they're nobody's fool. When people do take advantage of them, it's never without their inner consent and desire to be of service.

PISCES WITH **LIBRA** RISING

It's really not fair that so much charm, elegance, and grace should belong solely to one individual, yet the Pisces with Libra rising can't help but possess bucketfuls of all these qualities. Delightful to look at, these Pisceans give the impression of having stepped right out of the pages of a fairytale book; even if they're dressed in rags it's impossible for them to hide their special magic. Yet these people don't see themselves that way. Though they can dream up a rich fantasy better than most and can attract more suitors than anyone has the right to expect, there's often a deep-seated modesty and lack of confidence about them that stops them from believing in their own myth. Despite their delicate appearance, they are dedicated workers, who possess a gentle touch and have a peaceful, calming presence.

They have a gift for making others feel at ease, and this attribute is often worked into their vocation. They are idealistic, almost to a fault. If the beauty they see and feel inside themselves isn't reflected in their outside world, they can become disillusioned and confused, yet they're also capable of just waiting for the tide to change and the sun to shine again.

PISCES WITH **SCORPIO** RISING

Although Pisceans with Scorpio rising give the impression of subtle power and quiet command, they are actually very playful, amusing, and highly creative individuals. They have a way of gently but powerfully persuading people, which makes them excellent reformers. They can, indeed, be very influential when they express their likes and dislikes, and can cause others to jump to do their bidding. They are sometimes creative in the way they use their occasionally acid tongue to put people in their place. However, they're also sociable, generous, and totally fascinating in a mysterious, slightly dangerous way. Their captivating qualities attract the attention of many admirers. If this kind of appeal could be bottled and sold, many an actor would queue up to buy it! They are intensely focused both when speaking and listening, which is part of the reason why others are so gripped by their presence. They have sex appeal, charisma, and a wry smile that inspires and awes people at the same time. Their laserlike way of looking into people's souls can be a little unnerving but they are only searching, in everyone's best interests, for ways to understand them.

PISCES WITH **SAGITTARIUS** RISING

Humorous, expansive, and incapable of even seeing any limitation let alone being confined by it, the Pisces with Sagittarius rising appears to be a free spirit in the truest sense of the word. In fact, these Pisceans may have such a difficult time accepting any type of restriction that they occasionally go overboard and indulge in every conceivable form of pleasure. As a consequence, they frequently need to take time out to rest and be coddled in the comfort of a cozy, quiet home. But thanks to their jovial personality, they'll still be making light of the situation, cracking jokes, and making other people smile. Laughter is their therapy, and if they aren't laughing with others, they'll do it on their own just the same! They are generally optimistic and happy, and they are a cheerful, inspiring presence. However, for all their outward bravado and desire to see the world as well as experience everything in it, there's a very strong streak of traditionalism running through their veins. The loving bonds with their family will constantly call these sensitive Pisceans back to where they really feel secure, but not for long. They are restless people who always strive to indulge their wanderlust.

PISCES WITH **CAPRICORN** RISING

There's something very inflexible and controlled about the outward demeanor of the Pisces with Capricorn rising; however, they aren't really like that at all! They're highly intelligent and they have excellent communication skills, yet they're also willing to go with the flow and take life as it comes. It all stems from their innate wisdom, which would normally take other people many years to acquire. Their depth of imagination and their skill in conveying information mean that they have a talent for writing both fiction and nonfiction. They know the value of laughter as well as tears; they recognize that while life can be difficult, if only people were willing to have a good giggle, they would discover that wondrous, often hilarious irony that lightens the load. These are action-oriented people who take their endeavors seriously despite their humorous streak and their inherent gentleness. They approach their responsibilities earnestly, as though they were on a mission, and they move through life with authoritative grace. They are respected in both social and professional circles as people you can trust and rely on.

PISCES WITH **AQUARIUS** RISING

The Pisces with Aquarius rising is quite the entrepreneur, possessing a vision that is both imaginative and inventive. These individuals can apply this vision in many ways, sometimes to achieve a cherished goal of material gain but, more often, simply for the satisfaction they get from being charged up and from producing a constant flow of new, exciting, and workable ideas. The money is secondary; it's no more than a by-product. Their entrepreneurial skills mean that when they see a need for something that will benefit or entertain the public, they immediately see how to supply it. They are very sociable creatures but their real talent lies in being able to plug in, turn on, and tune in to humanity on a global scale. Intellectual acumen combined with emotional and intuitive understanding enable them to exist in the realms of the spiritual and material concurrently—heaven and earth personified! They are modest about their talents even though others are quick to praise and admire them. They have an active social life and make friends quickly and easily for they are so friendly and likable.

PISCES WITH **PISCES** RISING

Gentle, amusing, and enthusiastic, double Pisceans may seem to be living in their own world, but it's a world that they've created for themselves and they swim through it with a positive attitude. They enjoy discovering new and interesting perspectives from which to view life in its entirety, so the company of other people with their differing ideas provides them will all manner of pleasure. It's almost impossible for them to be bored because, beside the fact that they often bite off more than they can chew, they cherish those moments when they can sit in silence and think through all the inspired thoughts that are flowing in their heads. They are real dreamers and they have an uncanny way of conjuring up their own existence from their imaginations and, seemingly, making it real. Or is it that they're able to see so accurately into the future that they often seem to know what's going to happen next? Either way, they quite naturally get their information from another level of existence, which, to others can be a little scary! These are creative, talented people, who have much to show the rest of the world.

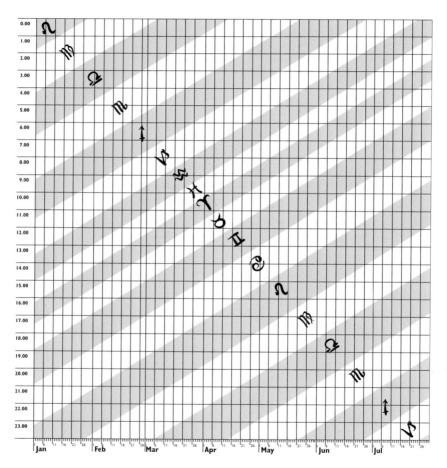

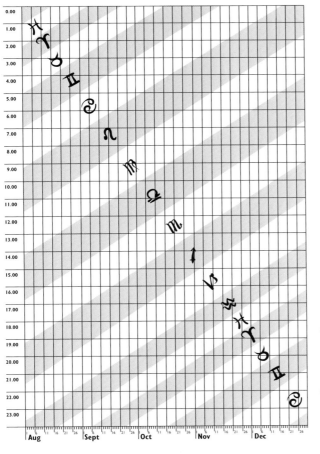

rising sign
TABLE

New York

latitude 39N00
meridian 75W00

♈	aries	♎	libra
♉	taurus	♏	scorpio
♊	gemini	♐	sagittarius
♋	cancer	♑	capricorn
♌	leo	♒	aquarius
♍	virgo	♓	pisces

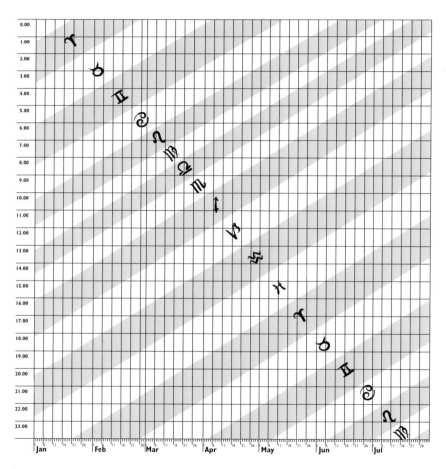

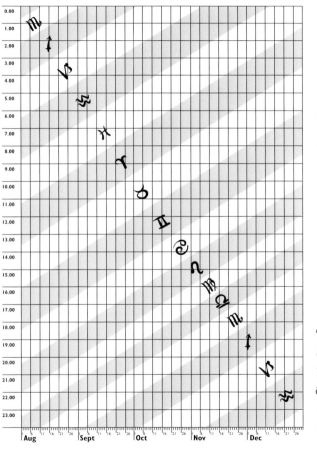

RISING SIGN
TABLE

Sydney

latitude 34S00
meridian 150E00

♈ aries   ♎ libra

♉ taurus   ♏ scorpio

♊ gemini   ♐ sagittarius

♋ cancer   ♑ capricorn

♌ leo   ♒ aquarius

♍ virgo   ♓ pisces

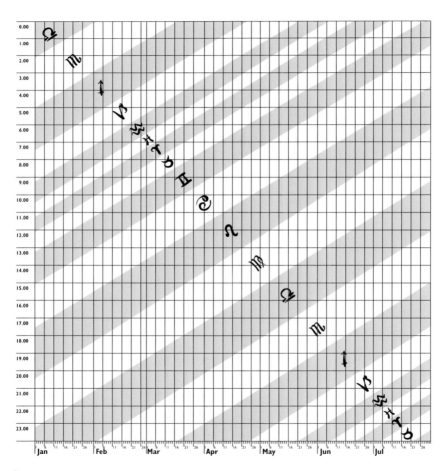

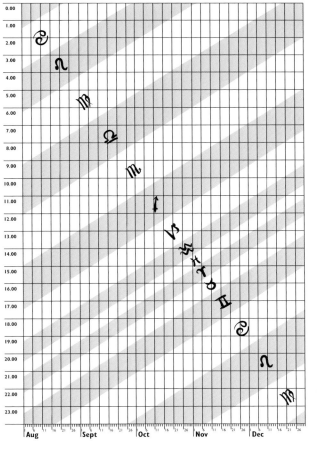

RISING SIGN
TABLE

London
latitude 51N30
meridian 0W00

♈ aries   ♎ libra
♉ taurus   ♏ scorpio
♊ gemini   ♐ sagittarius
♋ cancer   ♑ capricorn
♌ leo   ♒ aquarius
♍ virgo   ♓ pisces

PART THREE
RELATIONSHIPS

THE PISCES FRIEND

The basically shy, modest nature of Pisces doesn't make these people appear to be the most effusive and enthusiastic of friends, but they genuinely enjoy the company of others and are extremely kind, considerate, and sympathetic. They are also very good listeners and are often full of sage advice for those with whom they form caring, friendly relationships. At times, they can be totally wrapped up in their own world, while at others, they can be so incredibly selfless that it's heartbreaking to see. Their otherworldliness is very appealing if a little confusing, for most people are never quite sure where they stand or figure in Pisces' scheme of things. What they have to remember is that Pisceans have no scheme but are incredibly fluid in their attitude to life; as long as they smile, joke, and appear relaxed, then that person should be in no doubt that Pisces considers them a friend.

There's also a delightfully silly side to Pisces; they can find something to laugh about in almost everything. However, thanks to their supersensitivity, they are easily hurt by criticism, offhand remarks, and thoughtlessness. When a friend hurts them, Pisceans will silently withdraw and suddenly be unavailable until enough time has passed to allow their wounds to heal. Once that has happened, the friendship can resume and the friend won't ever be aware of what was said or done to upset their Pisces pal.

PISCES WITH **ARIES**

Aries has a limited attention span while Pisces has a limited amount of bubbly energy. After a while, Pisceans can seem moody but really it's because they need to be alone to recharge their batteries. Aries can easily hurt Pisces' feelings, whereas Pisces can be over-accommodating to Aries. All in all, Aries needs to be more sensitive and Pisces less so. Because Pisces and Aries are next to one another in the zodiac, it's likely that each has planets in the sign of the other, and if this is the case, they'll have more in common than is immediately apparent.

PISCES WITH **TAURUS**

Taurus can be a little stubborn, rigid, and opinionated while the flowing intellect of Pisces shows no bounds. This is a discrepancy that can cause a few problems but nothing that can't be overcome. Pisces is usually happy to go along with what Taurus suggests because the Bull has a real ability to make the Fish feel comfortable and happy. They have similar needs and wants in the sense that both like to find the easy route in most situations and both appreciate peace and quiet. Pisces's mutability helps to break down the inflexibility that Taurus is known for, so they'll naturally seek out the middle ground and reach the perfect agreement.

PISCES WITH GEMINI

Pisces and Gemini have adaptability and friendliness in common, which could take them a long way as acquaintances. They can get along pretty nicely on a superficial level, but if Pisces attempts to get beneath the surface, as Pisces likes to do, Gemini will become defensive. There aren't many things that unnerve a Gemini, but being unable to use logic to explain the intuitive tendency of a Pisces mind is one, and that's when Gemini can get agitated. However, these two will fascinate one another because, though they have much in common, they also have plenty that is not just different, but totally unrecognizable to the other.

PISCES WITH CANCER

Cancer makes a great buddy for Pisces. Not many people can understand the mysterious nature of Pisces, least of all Pisceans themselves, but Cancer comes very close. Both being a "feelings" type of person, they'll easily tune into one another. But if Cancer gets too moody, Pisces might just do a vanishing act, and if Pisces gets a little too unreliable, good old reliable Cancer will be furious. On the whole, though, these two will enjoy being in each other's company and will always find reasons to spend more time together.

PISCES WITH **LEO**

This is an intriguing friendship, for each will raise questions in the other that only the questioner will have the answers to. But this basic lack of understanding between them is no barrier to their camaraderie because, occasionally, they will turn on lights for the other that will illuminate new ways of thinking and of seeing the world. At first, Pisces might shy away from the outgoing Leo and Leo might be worried about disturbing the contemplative Pisces, but when they do start to talk, it could be hard to pull them apart. Once contact has been made, both will find that they have so much to discover about human nature.

PISCES WITH **VIRGO**

These are both thoughtful, gentle people who will find that they have much in common. Although their perspectives are diametrically opposed—Pisces is concerned with ultimate freedom in the emotional and spiritual realms, and Virgo with organization and understanding in the physical realm—both are flexible enough to make space for their interests to align and to establish a mutually fascinating friendship. In fact, their individual extremes might even begin to rub off on one another, which will bring them both a better balance between chaos and order. Virgo and Pisces have a natural affinity and affection for one another; this will mean a lifelong link.

PISCES WITH **LIBRA**

In certain situations, for instance where the champagne flows freely, these two will delight in each other's company and will find many things to talk about and empathize with. At other, more sober moments, though, while they'll respect each other's position, the conversation could go a little flat. Pisces likes to go off at a tangent, exploring the surreal aspects of life and sometimes diving into its depths, particularly when it comes to emotional issues, while Libra prefers to skim the surface, remaining light-hearted and being careful to avoid those uncomfortable dark corners of human consciousness.

PISCES WITH **SCORPIO**

Pisces and Scorpio really connect, and because they feel a natural rapport they're able to let their hair down and have some seriously amusing, creative fun together. Pisces is elusive and Scorpio is secretive, yet their sympathy for and sensitivity to each other are such that they share an exclusivity that's a complete mystery to everyone around them. Even if they don't see each other for months, or even years, they'll quickly get reacquainted when they meet again and will get on together as if they had never spent any time apart. They'll have an easy liking for one another, but the friendship is likely to go deeper than that.

PISCES WITH **SAGITTARIUS**

As friends, these two really click. They can share boundless fun when they're out on the town together. They have a way of daring one another to do really audacious things, and if their mothers only knew what they were up to, they'd be ordered home immediately! On the other hand, with their two heads together, they could accomplish great, courageous feats. Their conversations can be silly or serious, but what's sure is that they'll both enter into them in the right spirit. They even find their arguments enjoyable because they'll expand each other's perspective with their different takes on life. Both having a jovial and generous streak; these two are an inspiration to one another and make great pals.

PISCES WITH **CAPRICORN**

What a fertile friendship this can be! Somehow neither is put off by, but rather enjoys, the differences between them, namely imaginative, emotional idealism versus sound, practical reality. Pisces' no-holds-barred approach encourages Capricorn to let go of the sense of responsibility that can stop them from having fun, while Capricorn provides the type of solid camaraderie that doesn't drift away. Between them, one thing leads to another—Pisces will come up with ideas and Capricorn will help to make them concrete. They work in tandem in order to create a wonderful reality for themselves and for those around them.

PISCES WITH **AQUARIUS**

This is a case of two heads are better than one. There's little to disagree about when these two get together; in fact there's plenty to agree on and then develop. It would only take an evening for these two to be on track for solving the mysteries of the world. They have amazing conversations together and both have a compelling interest in what the other has to say, but just as things get rolling and Aquarius is beginning to get fascinated by it all, Pisces might start to drift off mentally to another plane. The conversation could fizzle out completely unless Pisces returns to reality pretty quickly.

PISCES WITH **PISCES**

Two friends born under the sign of Pisces could be so in sympathy with each other that they'll catch each other's drift without the need to talk or, when they do get verbal, they'll frequently finish each other's sentences. These two have a natural curiosity about one another but the level of comfort they feel within themselves as individuals will be reflected in their level of compatibility. Contrarily, they could also be two Fish swimming in opposite directions, and not even vaguely interested in each other. Such is the nature of this enigmatic sign; sometimes these two will really hit it off, and sometimes not at all, and no one really knows why.

THE **PISCES WOMAN** IN LOVE

The unfathomable emotions of the Pisces woman give her the type of elusive mystery that makes most men want to follow her about, no matter how vain their attempts to truly possess her might prove. She has something so ultrafeminine about her—a combination of sensitivity, gentleness, and selfless compassion—that men are irresistibly drawn to her. Her femininity massages their egos and makes them feel totally masculine. Where love is concerned, she's romantic and idealistic, and she spreads her net wide in the hope of picking up the perfect fairytale lover on her radar screen. She doesn't behave aggressively; she simply wants to be open to the possibility of romantic bliss. She longs to meet and merge completely with her soul mate and will never lose heart, no matter how many times she's disappointed along the way, for she has an unfailing faith in the ecstasy of true love.

Many men will pick up on her openness and empathy, and will think that she's pliable and easily molded into their ideal woman. However, although she may be capable of compliance and subservience in the name of love, she will, in essence, always remain beyond his reckoning. She'll quickly slip through the fingers of any man who thinks he has her in his grasp or who starts to take her for granted. Unless he proves as loving, devoted, and generous with his heart as she is, Lady Pisces is capable of doing a vanishing act before his very eyes. She'll simply melt away, first mentally, then emotionally, and finally physically. She needs to be treated with tenderness and sensitivity, but she'll also find it near-impossible to fall in love with a man who acts like a doormat and who lays down his dignity for her to walk all over. Her man must be a real man in every sense of the word, capable of deep passion and with a strong character. She needs someone she can look up to and respect, but who also respects her in return.

When she's truly in love the Pisces woman is as happy and playful as a dolphin leaping and diving through the waves. Her sense of delight makes her feel inspired and inspiring; it's almost impossible to wipe the smile from her face or contain her wondrous creativity. With this woman, the world becomes a magical, amusing, and fun place to be, and since she now wants for nothing, she'll lay nothing less than all she has, including her devotion, support, and intuitive wisdom, at the feet of the person to whom she's given her heart. But a greedy man would be wise to remember that all these riches come at a price; he must be capable of dreaming her dreams, cherishing her emotionally and physically, and being prepared to offer nothing less than his soul in return.

PISCES WOMAN WITH **ARIES MAN**

 In love: The attraction between the fiery Aries man and the fairytale Piscean princess is tangible. He is flattered to his chivalrous masculine core by her initial submissiveness, which isn't all that it appears, but he'll want to see it that way. His energy just carries her along and she's happy to go with his flow—at first. It's thrilling, passionate, and inspiring for both of them to be traveling along this idealized path, but if they stay on that journey for very long, they'll realize that it cannot be sustained. Idealism must make way for reality otherwise she will have no say in where they're going and he'll be terribly disappointed when he turns around one day to find that she has vanished. Communication is a key issue between these two and if they can successfully convey their feelings and expectations to one another, they might just have a match made in heaven. The Aries man is so masculine and the Pisces woman so feminine that it's easy to see why these two feel so right together. And besides, the sex is great! But he may not be able to value her more elusive and imaginative qualities and every once in a while, he'll trample on her delicate feelings, forcing her to withdraw and become even more remote. But there is hope, and it's worth persevering, especially if he makes an effort to develop a little more sensitivity and if she tries to let things roll off her more readily. This could be a long-lasting relationship, but compromise is certainly needed.

In bed: He's hot, she's ready, and together this makes one steamy love affair. Sexuality is one aspect of the relationship that could keep them together long after other connections have dwindled away. They may no longer be speaking to one another, but that won't get in the way of a good romp. The Pisces woman and Aries man can whip each other up into a sweaty frenzy, which is so sexy and satisfying that both are left literally breathless and stunned by the awesome pleasure they've experienced. She will intuitively push the right buttons on him, and his instinctive drive will propel her straight into that ethereal realm of ecstatic bliss. One thing to realize, though, is that the Pisces woman might not be entirely present. She is certainly there in body, and is capable of going through exactly the right motions to make herself his ideal bedmate. But her soul exists on another plane and her mind could simply be elsewhere. The truth is that the reason why she so enjoys herself and loses herself so completely in the sexual act is because while she's doing it, there's a parallel world going on inside her head where she imagines the perfect lovemaking. The Aries man will be there to bring this parallel world into the real one, but if she thinks for one moment that his passion doesn't truly reflect his deeper emotions, the whole fantasy will probably come to an end. Trust is a key ingredient. Without it, she'll withhold everything she would otherwise wholeheartedly share with him.

PISCES WOMAN WITH **TAURUS MAN**

In love: Here is a love that the Pisces woman can trust. It looks like the one she's been waiting for all her life. He's romantic, protective, and so much like a real prince. And the Pisces woman appears to have all that the Taurus man could want…he thinks that he has finally found someone he can control! He'll have to think again, but she won't let him know that she has a mind of her own; he'll have to figure it out for himself. Meanwhile, he has all the strength and sensitivity she requires in a man and he is so susceptible to her dreamy, romantic allure that it won't take her long to capture his heart completely. She'll enjoy being spoiled by a Taurus man who simply adores buying her flowers and chocolates, and taking her away for romantic weekends. But that first flush of romance is not going to last forever, for then up steps Mr. Practicality—the man who wants to save his money by keeping her barefoot and pregnant in the kitchen, and making the meals for which he has set the table so beautifully. If she longs for security, then she'll happily submit because she knows that there will still be occasions when he'll whisk her off to a wonderful restaurant where she can dress up and relive her dream. But some Pisces ladies will feel that the bubble has burst and will be totally disillusioned with the loss of their romantic ideals. If the Pisces woman does decide to give her heart to him, he'll treasure it beyond measure.

In bed: When this relationship becomes sexual—and it won't take long—that's when it really becomes a relationship. She can have him on his knees with just a glance—a very convenient position as far as she's concerned—and he might even make a proposal (indecent or otherwise!) while he's down there. These two should get a big, firm mattress and heaps of feather cushions, because they'll be spending a lot of time in the bedroom. This is where they can achieve an intimacy that's both comforting and fulfilling. They will adore being enveloped in their private world and wrapped around each other's bodies. It's the physical closeness that is so important to the Taurus man, and the emotional connection that anchors the Pisces woman's heart. Any time that other aspects of the relationship are breaking down, blissful togetherness between the sheets will halt the damage and make their love blossom all over again. She is more than willing to give herself up and be totally immersed in his strongly sensual needs. She has such an erotic imagination that he might fear losing himself in her soft naked body, yet it also gives him a sense of the strength of his masculinity. Her total surrender makes him an even more ardent and skillful lover—and that suits her just fine.

PISCES WOMAN WITH GEMINI MAN

 In love: The Pisces woman and Gemini man appear to float and flow around each other in a delightful dance. They both like to look at life in a variety of ways; his thoughts are lateral while hers have depth, so together they've got all the moves covered. She intrigues and confuses him, which he finds a devastatingly appealing combination. He's always good fun to have around and loves a puzzle, particularly one that's as mystifying as the Pisces woman, but unless he's able to figure her out, at least partially, he could get distracted by something that is more logical and more understandable. In her view he somehow appears flippant and superficial; his words suggest understanding but his actions lack conviction. Her super-sensitivity can make him feel as though he's walking on eggshells and that, for a man who usually trips through life lightly, is rather nerve-racking, so something in this pairing will never quite click. Neither of them should dive into this relationship headfirst; it might be wiser just to paddle about until something better comes along. It all depends on whether they're both prepared to make a continual effort, but it's unlikely that either of them could stay in the relationship for long unless the Gemini man can stay silent and tune into her depth of feeling, at least long enough to get into her and into the experience of really making love. The other option is for the Pisces woman to adapt to his constant need to verbalize, and just savor her moments alone when she can enjoy some peace.

In bed: There's an instant sexual attraction between these two, but it has a quizzical quality rather than a rampant, passionate one. Just about anything inspires the curiosity of the Gemini man. Both of them feel the thrill of possibility, and that can be enough of an aphrodisiac to get them as far as the bedroom. Once there, the Pisces woman could really tickle his fancy. He adores her flowing sensuality, her inspired touch, and the way that she drifts dreamily into his arms, but the Gemini man is more likely to get off from hearing her sexual fantasies than from actually making them come true. It's probable that her fantasies would raise rather more than just the hairs on his back, but she won't want to divulge her secrets to someone who might not be around for long. Sounds like a bit of a disappointment? Maybe, but he's also very clever and agile and might sweep down on her without any prior warning. And when that happens, he'll prove to her how talented he really is.

PISCES WOMAN WITH CANCER MAN

 In love: This is a beautiful, precious, perfect love. Emotionally, the Pisces lady and the Cancer man give and receive in equal proportions, spiritually, physically, and mentally. Things could hardly be better and since both are Water signs, they meld and flow into one another. When the world feels a little threatening and all she wants is someone to hold her, he'll be there, and when he needs to forget about his troubles, she can take him out of himself with her love. The only problem is that they could get so caught up in their own private world that things of a more practical nature are ignored. But the Cancer man will be there to gently bring them back to reality and, strangely, he's never so crabby when he's around her. If he does get into a mood, she'll be able to look beyond it and carry on as usual, knowing that it will pass as surely as the tides will change.

In fact, she's so inclined to drift off into her own dreamy realms, she may not even have noticed his bad mood in the first place and this, most of the time, is what her Cancer man would prefer. While these two are floating away on their fluffy pink clouds to the sound of angels singing, they'll need to spare a thought for the mere mortals of the world. Once they've found each other, they'll never want to let go. This is as close to perfect as it can get.

 In bed: This is transcendental sex, the most uplifting sort of sensuality! These two find themselves having an out-of-body experience every time their very real bodies are writhing together on the bed. They've found their perfect partner in passion and it's enough to make them weep for joy. Is this an exaggeration? Not at all! If they go out to friends for dinner, they'll either make their excuses and leave early so they can be alone, or else they'll sneak off to the bathroom at the same time. When they eventually float back to the dining table, the look on their faces will confirm to everyone exactly what they've been up to—and they won't even be embarrassed! They're always blissfully unaware of anyone else when the other is in the room. The spirit of this relationship is intoxicating and the physical side is heart-stopping. Yes, he does like to have deep roots planted in the ground and she likes to flow free, but this difference works to their advantage. She won't let him get away with his usual conventionality, and he'll love it, and he simply won't let her get away.

PISCES WOMAN WITH **LEO MAN**

In love: The Leo man will completely dazzle the Pisces woman. She's like the damsel in distress but this time it's the Lion who's coming to save her. He'll play the true gallant, sweeping her off her feet and showing her the time of her life. It won't always be like that, however. She loves the display of strength that he so willingly puts on, but she's also deceptively strong and when he's feeling vulnerable, she won't fail to be there to lift his spirits. His generosity and warmth will overwhelm her, while she'll fascinate and intrigue him so much that he will pursue her with a single-minded passion that she can't fail to be flattered by. She has what he admires and wants in a partner—alluring sensuality, romance, and imagination. The Lady Fish is rather shy but a Leo man has enough confidence for both of them. He prefers to be the one who shines and she's content with that. Both have their own brand of magic and when they're together, life will feel romantic and otherworldly, but not all that glitters is gold—they might occasionally need to take a reality check! These two could blind themselves to the more difficult aspects of their relationship for quite a while, but eventually, unless they make an effort to stay connected, those difficulties will become glaringly obvious. Her tendency to drift when not fully mentally engaged will drive the Lion wild; he expects her to think about nothing but him.

In bed: Passionate, ardent, adoring lover meets poetic, romantic, emotional mate. Sounds like a recipe for bliss in the bedroom, especially if their bed is large enough to make believe it's a stage. These two will love performing for one another: one could read from an erotic novel and the other could act it out; a dance or love song might be on the program, or even a striptease. But what's really cooking between these two? The Pisces woman brings out the predatory, animal nature of her Lion lover, so she shouldn't be surprised to find herself fighting him off with a chair and a whip, but in truth, she has a remarkable talent for taming him. Her soft, dreamy sensuality most definitely evokes curiosity in this cat and he'll take care to paw at her delicately so that his enormous passion won't frighten her away. What he doesn't know is that she's extremely excited by his lust and enjoys teasing him into an even greater state of impatience and arousal. This Lady Fish would love to be consumed by his Leo fire; she would happily sacrifice her body on the pyre of his passion but she knows no bounds, so even the voracious appetite of the king of beasts may not be enough to bring her fulfillment.

PISCES WOMAN WITH **VIRGO MAN**

In love: The Pisces woman just knows that there's more to this guy than meets the eye, and there's certainly more than he's willing to reveal. But she's the girl who can ease her way around his detachment and help to unlock his emotions—and boy, does he need help!

So does she when it comes to all those practical, mundane matters that he's so good at; this gentle guy can help to ground her in reality and stop her drifting about. This makes for a very nice arrangement. What he lacks, she has more than enough of and what she lacks, he has in sackfuls. As opposite signs of the zodiac they complement each other perfectly, but he may not be very willing to share all he has with the Lady Fish at first—he's very good at compartmentalizing the separate areas of his life, while she needs to flow through it all unhindered. At worst, this could lead to a deadly silence between them; if she feels that he's keeping things from her then she may not be willing to share her secrets with him and so he'll miss out on all the wondrous experiences that these two could have together. So long as she doesn't take his initial reticence and criticisms too much to heart, and so long as he doesn't try to meddle in those areas of her life where she prefers to float free, then their love could grow not only into a thing of beauty, but into something that heals all ills and soothes all pain.

 In bed: The earthy Virgo man can take a little while to get going in the bedroom because he's often shy, but the Pisces woman understands shyness. Once she goes to work on him he'll get going very quickly—and keep right on going. He can be insatiable with the right lover, and it just so happens that she's the one. They fit together like a hand in a glove. Together, they are pure, pulsating passion, which is a pleasant surprise for them both. These two may not hit it off on the first try, but because they have a sort of compulsion to be together, they'll probably try again and again, and each time it will simply get more explosive. There will be moments when the Pisces woman feels as though she's naked in a field of wild flowers on a hot summer afternoon—excited yet enraptured and enjoying a delightfully naughty sense of freedom. Being with her when she's like this will make the Virgo man wild with desire. Fantasy turns into reality when a Pisces woman turns to her Virgo man for sex. This relationship is very erotic, amazingly spiritual, sweetly emotional, and unbelievably satisfying.

PISCES WOMAN WITH **LIBRA MAN**

In love: The Pisces woman and Libra man could be the most heart-stoppingly romantic couple that ever existed. They're equally loving and he's very good at doing all those little things that a girl expects from her partner. Their relationship is pure heaven. It's floating-away-on-gossamer-wings time, with harps serenading the happy couple as they drift up into paradise. These two will always remember the song that was playing when they first gazed at each other across a crowded room and they'll play it on anniversaries and whenever they feel romantic, which will probably be rather often. Eventually, however, it will feel as if that song is the only thing keeping them together for, while he spends a lot of time thinking and talking about their relationship, she might be the only one who truly invests in it emotionally. They might not get exactly what they need from each other unless she can play it cool and really mean it, and he can be a little more emotionally involved and really mean it, too. That might be asking too much, despite the promising start to the relationship. However, the love they share is very real and there's no reason why it shouldn't last. It all depends on how they play it; if they stay in the now, the relationship could work, but they may not have the capacity to grow together as many couples do.

 In bed: When it's time for a little lovin' with the lights down low, the Libra man wants everything to be perfect for his sweet Pisces lady. So that means a scented bubble bath followed by her putting on her silky lingerie. And she shouldn't forget to put her hair up too because he's always wanted to do that thing where he takes the pins out and she shakes her head while looking up at him adoringly! She can play this game of allure better than most women and the naughty little things he says and does to excite her erotic desires make it all so arousing. There'll be times when she'd prefer him to do and say big things, like pick her up and throw her on the bed like a damsel in distress at the hands of the wicked villain. She simply has to tell him the fantasy and he'll be happy to oblige, though of course, that rather takes away the element of surprise. Next time he hopes to excite her with this scenario, she'll have some other fantasy in mind, which all goes to show that, because Libra man uses his head and not his heart to probe her mysterious secrets, the way to this girl's pleasure continually eludes him. Still, if he doesn't mind the chase, she certainly won't mind trying to get away.

Pisces Woman with **Scorpio Man**

 In love: The Scorpio man is passionately possessive and sexually jealous where the Pisces lady is concerned. If he could have his way, she'd be tied to the bed and strapped into a chastity belt when he's out. If he earns her trust, she'll do as he asks simply because he gives her what she really wants—good loving, great sex, and a sense of strength and security. He'll never find a woman who's more agreeable to his demands; in fact, she might seem a little too wet to some men, but not to the Scorpio man. He knows exactly what to do with her and brings out the best in her by handling her supersensitivity to perfection. It's true that he can be somewhat manipulative, but she's wise to it and will either choose to flow with it, or simply around it. Her romanticism, far from being a shallow need for candlelit dinners and love tokens, opens up doors to a spiritual realm that he longs to explore. He wants to delve deeply into the Pisces lady and reach the parts that other men simply cannot reach. These two won't even need to talk about it to know that there's a huge dose of magic in the feelings that they evoke in one another. This partnership works very well; all the elements necessary for a merging of heart and soul are present. There may never be another relationship quite like this one for emotional intensity.

 In bed: The Pisces lady has been dreaming about her knight in shining armor from a very young age. She's always known that one day she'd meet a man who could burst the dam of her fathomless sexuality. Well, here comes Mr. Scorpio. He's that man, so get ready to burst! Meanwhile, all he wants is a woman who's not frightened off by his powerful sex drive. And here she is! She's not totally aware of what she's walking into but her naive trust allows her to experience fully the wonders of what the Scorpio man has to offer. Other women can leave him feeling like a cold mountain stream, but a sensual sex session with the Lady Fish turns him into a bubbling, steaming-hot geyser! Old Faithful will seem like nothing more than a dripping faucet compared to them. Mr. Scorpio's intensity moves her in deep places and she won't be able to drift away unless he gives her permission because his sexual prowess will keep on luring her back for more. Her erotic creativity will mystify him so much that he'll have to use all his penetrating powers of detection to solve the puzzle that she poses. There'll be many "Eureka!" moments along the way to them reaching their final conclusion. It's rare to find such mutually fulfilling sexual chemistry between two people; they could write the book of hot love. Although both Scorpio and Pisces are subtle signs, the dirty grins that they'll wear when they're with one another will say it all!

PISCES WOMAN WITH SAGITTARIUS MAN

In love: The Pisces woman and Sagittarius man will be drawn together by a feeling for the possibility of endless love. "Ordinary" isn't a word that describes either of them, so theirs could be an extraordinary love affair. They'll both enjoy long, fascinating conversations about the meaning of life and about what we're all doing here, but no matter what conclusions they come to, they may not be able to answer the question of why they're together. He doesn't like her getting under his skin, which she'll do in spite of him because he finds her so enticing and intriguing, and although she's hopelessly attracted to his fun-loving, adventurous soul, he's always taking himself off and simply isn't there enough for her. Every time he leaves she feels she has to extricate her heart; he's completely cavalier about her emotions. At first, they'll drive each other crazy with desire but eventually they'll just drive each other crazy. At this point, they'd be wise to stand back and take stock of what there is between them. It's hard to deny that they feel strong passions for each other and that both of them have a leaning toward the spiritual and philosophical. If they can take a few small leaps of faith, then this is a partnership that could have a firm foundation of love, hope, mind, and body, but without some spirit it will be hard to maintain.

 In bed: He's a fun guy for a romp in the hay, a tumble in the grass, or a roll in the sack, so she'll never get bored with the scenery when she's frolicking around with a Sagittarius man. But sex for the Pisces woman isn't always a picnic. She's the romantic type who needs all the pretty trimmings to achieve true satisfaction. When they get together between the sheets, she'd like a little more emotional connection. He'll give her something of what she needs but the experience may be shorter lived than she expects! He's not really the luxuriating type; although he'll be seduced by her soft, languorous sensuality, he isn't very subtle in expressing his arousal. She wants to feel his passion, deeply, and is excited by his obvious desire for her, but while she's happy to give herself up to him, she won't like having her feelings trampled on. These two can enjoy their sexy fun and games as long as the sun shines, but should be ready to pack up when they see the dark clouds approaching. They should accept the dynamic of their immense sexual desire and capacity for one another, and treat it like an ever-changing, developing part of their relationship. In fact, neither of them would ever get bored and things would simply get better.

PISCES WOMAN WITH **CAPRICORN MAN**

 In love: Love grows steadily deeper, more enriching, and more intimate when Mr. Goat and Lady Fish spend time together. She can trust him with her heart and soul, for he's as steady as a rock and easy to cling to when she starts riding the waves of emotion. He longs to immerse himself in her and feel her soft, sensitive feelings washing all over him. In the Capricorn man, the Pisces lady has found the guy who can turn her dreams and fantasies into both practical and sensual reality. A strong sense of fulfillment accompanies this relationship; she needs his anchor and he needs taking out of himself, which she can do so well. She has a feminine allure that is highly intoxicating and seductive to this stern, self-contained man, for he secretly longs to feel total, abandoned love and he senses that this is the woman to help him do it. He can be a touch rigid and pedantic, which can put a strain on her more imaginative, dreamy nature, but she accepts and understands his reasons. He would be an especially wonderful, supportive partner for the Pisces woman with career ambitions because he'd really get involved and offer solid, practical help. The more time they spend together, the better this relationship gets. Their love could go on forever, and then for a little while longer.

 In bed: Happiness wells up inside him and comes tumbling out when these two sensual lovers make it together. It's quite a powerful thing to be able to do that to a man and it's down to the perfect sexual blend that exists between Mr. Capricorn and Ms. Pisces. She soothes him with her soft caresses and totally surrenders her body to his masterful application of erotic pleasure. She feels completely fulfilled by his masculinity, and thoroughly enjoys the sensation of his tightly coiled sexual intensity wrestling with his self-control. She enjoys it so much that she won't need to drift off into the nether realms of her imagination because he'll keep her fascinated and involved right to the point where he loses his battle. Reality is far more beautiful when she's with him. He's sexually insatiable and a little controlling, so if she feels like acting the sex slave, all she has to do is throw herself into the role and walk around naked, pandering to his every need—and then who really has the power? With the right combination of shy looks and wiggling hips she could soon have him following her around. These two adore one another, and sex in the most delectable positions brings them both to the point of worship. It's such an intoxicating cocktail of sensuality and eroticism that they'll be licking their lips to savor every last drop.

PISCES WOMAN WITH **AQUARIUS MAN**

 In love: When the Aquarius man meets Lady Pisces, he's full of wonder and curiosity because he's easily seduced by anything he can't figure out. He usually takes immense pride in his intellect but when the mysterious Pisces woman walks into his rational realm, he's completely bamboozled. She is eager to please and is drawn to his charismatic friendliness and sharp perception. Although mentally and spiritually they share some accord, when it comes to the emotional world, they are galaxies apart. But these two connect on the level of cosmic consciousness rather than on that of the mundane world. Given time, they can work together beautifully for the Aquarius man learns fast—even when it comes to learning not to try to figure her out—while she melds perfectly into his world—the way a lake hugs the rocks on a shore. However, she has to have faith that he is a rock, because he won't ever say so. That would be too much like committing himself to one single form of expression. Meanwhile, she needs to let the waters of her emotional ocean gently wash over him instead of trying to immerse him because, if she does, he'll just roll away. This Aquarius man is certainly loyal, but he needs all the space in the universe in order to express himself, his loyalty, and his love in his own way. These two will adore each other forever, but without trust that adoration will only exist on some other plane.

In bed: The Pisces woman will instinctively know whether or not the Aquarius man is for her the moment she lays eyes on him. In fact, there will be no prospect of love if she doesn't immediately feel some chemistry. Eternal intrigue is what keeps the Aquarius man interested, so he may hold back a bit to see if the electricity between them has the power to turn them both on and light up their libidos. However, if she's in any doubt, there's one surefire way to find out, and that's to strip off and jump in at the deep end. She'll either be left breathless and frantic for more lovemaking or desperate to pull out the bait. He's emotionally aloof while she rates a ten on the scale of romantic sensuality, so this could cause problems for the Lady Fish who wants to take her Water-Bearer lover deep down to swim in a limitless sea of erotic and emotional feeling. He can do erotic and limitless well enough, but for him it has to be on a stratospheric, fantasy level, high above the clouds, where he won't drown in pleasure but will be inspired by the stars he sees before his eyes. Sexually, this is an all-or-nothing coupling—all they have to do is try it once.

PISCES WOMAN WITH **PISCES MAN**

In love: These two could swim around each other for a long, long time before one of them gets around to making the first move. Both Pisces men and women are quite shy until they start sensing some mutual attraction and picking up the good vibrations between them. Both know the pain of loss and have a very sensitive, vulnerable side that needs protecting, so they'll have to earn each other's trust and feel safe with one another before they're ready to dive in together. Once they do, though, the relationship will be truly lovely. They're able to merge together so completely that they won't know where one stops and the other begins; it's as though they dissolve in each other's company. There'll be a lot of flip-flopping around of roles; one of them will be the helpful, healing partner one day and the selfish, needy one the next. There might be times when these two Fish get so lost in their exclusive dreamworld that it's difficult to fish them back out into mundane reality. They could be in for quite a shock when the real world drops its line down and hauls them out to face its demands. However, two Pisces lovers can keep the romance going in a relationship a lot longer than any other pairing; after all, another Pisces is about the closest each will get to someone who understands them. These two will empathize with each other and feel deeply for one another. With a healthy dose of practicality on top, they've got everything they need.

 In bed: Lovemaking between these two sexed-up Fish is pure poetry in motion. Their gliding movements are mutually soothing, hypnotic, and uplifting, and sweep through all their senses like an addictive drug. As they gracefully skim over, under, and through each other's bodies, their mesmerizing lovemaking lifts them both up above and far beyond the material plane of existence. They drift away in an endless sea of romantic, erotic delight and it's difficult to believe that any other lovers are capable of such heavenly intimacy. But that continuous, gentle, rocking motion could make them seasick, so one or both of them may need to inject a bit more dynamism into things. It wouldn't matter which it is, for both are wonderful actors, who can throw themselves fully into any role they wish to play, and either could easily get their imagination flowing along more raunchy paths. The sensual appetites of the Pisces man and Pisces woman are as vast as any ocean, so whipping up the swell until passion crashes over them in wave after wave is just another, more exciting, way of surfing their sexual pleasure. They'll dive deeply into underwater realms and try every which way that occurs to them. They don't need a manual; Pisces' imagination will dream up more positions, scenarios, and story lines than most people could even dream of. They can get themselves into trouble sometimes, but they're also masters at getting themselves off the hook.

THE **PISCES MAN** IN LOVE

The Pisces man cannot help but love deeply, idealistically, and sometimes painfully longingly, even though he rarely shows any of this on the surface. He's a quiet man, not like so many others who are full of bravado and who have the ladies lining up just to get a sniff of them. But this man is worth his weight in gold because once he meets the lady of his dreams, he'll give her everything and will bend over backward to keep her feeling happy, amorous, and free of stress. When he's in love, the dreamily romantic Pisces man falls head over heels, which is wonderful when the feeling is mutual—and with his trusting nature, he'll believe that it is. That's why he can easily be hurt and could wake up one day to discover that he was only deluding himself. While he was imagining that he was paying off the credit-card bills of a woman who really loved him for himself, that she was going to marry him, ride off into the future with him, and that the two of them would live happily ever after, she's left town, never to be seen again. At least she won't have any bad debts! Fortunately, the Pisces man doesn't bear a grudge. He'll forgive and forget, and may well meet another lady just like her, and may possibly make the same mistake again. Over time, though, once he's become jaded by life's harshness, he'll learn to be more cautious and to always be on his guard, which is a pity for he's a fine gentleman—loyal, loving, kind, supportive, giving—who really deserves the best.

The Pisces man also has what it takes to make a woman feel good about herself. He sees her as the ultimate in beauty and perfection, no matter what she looks like. Whether she's a beauty queen or rather homely, his romantic imagination colors his world and turns her into a picture of perfection. And anyway, he's not usually very fussy about appearances; he'll look into her heart and if it's as beautiful as he hopes it will be, then he'll regard her as absolutely gorgeous, sexy, and worthy of his worship. He's capable of writing her the most beautiful love letters ever—enough to make any woman's heart melt—and she'll find there's a delicate quality about him that reflects his inner sensitivity. Physically he's not much of a he-man, although there are exceptions that prove the rule.

Extremely funny when least expected, but also thoughtful, intelligent, and nonjudgmental, the Pisces man is not someone to take lightly. He does sometimes need to delve into gloomy, doom-laden worlds, and then he'd appreciate a lot of love and support, but there are also times when he's grateful for some solo contemplation. Then, as he sees it, he's not up to anything peculiar; he's only taking time out in order to visit the darker corners of his vast inner world.

PISCES MAN WITH **ARIES WOMAN**

 In love: The Pisces man will fulfill every fantasy of the Aries woman and he'll be whatever she wants him to be, whether that's a prince, a handyman, or a masseur. However, he requires loads of attention, appreciation, and affection in return. If she can provide these he'll be hers forever. If she can't, he may behave in one of two ways: either he'll follow her around like the lovesick puppy an Aries girl just can't abide, or he'll simply drift away and she'll never see him again. The Pisces man is fascinated by the single-minded energy with which an Aries woman approaches life. Part of him feels so connected to her, yet there is another side to him which is connected to no one and nothing or, better put, to everyone and everything. He's a chameleon-like lover and she'll be a sucker for his charm, which he possesses in bucketfuls, but she might just run for it when she grows tired of trying to figure him out. Realistically speaking, she might not possess the kind of refined qualities that he prefers a woman to have. As their signs are positioned next to one another in the zodiac, it's possible that they have some planets in common and in this case, the pairing could work out beautifully. If not, they could very well make an odd couple, he being dreamy and introspective, she focused and extrovert.

 In bed: If she needs to find out what's on his mind, the Aries girl will need to sum up all her directness and she must ask in the most explicit terms, because the Pisces man can be very ambiguous.

However, this man is able to create the ultimate sexual fantasy, with her in the starring role. He's into feet and she's into heads, so together they could write their own version of the Kama Sutra. He has the ability to bring out the Aries woman's secret desire to feel soft and feminine. The dreamy way he envelops her in his romantic lovemaking has her longing to play the femme fatale. Her raw desires and pure passion have him feeling like an all-powerful super sex god. There's only one slight problem, though. He wants her to be a softly sensual feminine lady, just as she needs him to be the powerful dominant man she can look up to. If things aren't working out as though they were the stars of a romantic film, he might do a vanishing act. He's an elusive guy so if the Aries woman's attention has waned and her head is turned, he'll be with someone else before she knows it. Neither will ever fully understand the other. Although these two are very different creatures, if they're happy to remain in a state of flux, their relationship could work out well, as it has some very positive things going for it.

PISCES MAN WITH **TAURUS WOMAN**

In love: On the whole, the Taurus woman is level-headed and practical, and the Pisces man, although a very capable human being, is somewhat impractical and dreamy. The two seem like opposites at first, but in fact, they fit together like spoons. She will forget all her own practical aims once she mixes with the Fish; he helps her to float out of herself and this isn't such a bad thing. Where the Taurus woman has focus, the Pisces man looks at life through a prism, seeing the myriad possibilities in every situation. It would be easy for her to get drawn into his world and never come out of it, but would she really want to? For short spells of time, she's okay with that, and, in fact, finds it rather liberating and exciting. He provides a certain amount of romantic, emotional nourishment, but she's most comfortable on solid ground, which is where she really flourishes. Meanwhile, he'll benefit from her uncluttered vision and sense of direction: she can provide him with an elegant and comfortable container for the safe-keeping of his dreams. They each have strengths in areas where the other is lacking, and a mutual recognition of this fact makes for a pair of sympathetic lovers. Where this couple really align is in the realm of romance: their bodies and souls both feed on it. He will show her wonders and delights that capture her imagination just as she will arouse his physical senses with her intimate knowledge of pleasure. This is what binds them together and makes it difficult to pull them apart.

 In bed: The problem for these two will be getting out of bed. For a Piscean man it's his number one domain—the place where he could live, eat, breathe, and work. He is an odd mixture of selfish and selfless, so if the Lady Taurus doesn't mind crumbs and beer cans littering the bed, he'll treat her to an unforgettable voyage from seduction to erogenous ecstasy. He has the sort of imagination that could make an ocean look shallow, so there will never be a dull moment in bed and he will happily spend hours on end in playful splashing. But the Pisces man is also sensitive, so when the Taurus woman has had enough and tells him so, he may feel hurt. However, this is unlikely to happen very often, because Lady Taurus has the stamina to outlast even the most ardent lover. What may cause her a few insecure moments, though, is his tendency to drift away on his own stream of dreams. She needs to feel her man up close and personal in every sense of the word. He tends not to verbalize but he needs his woman to do so with the sweetest, softest murmurs, which is something Lady Taurus knows how to do. She's not shy about expressing her needs and desires and this will encourage him to rise to the occasion and will make him more solid and dependable.

PISCES MAN WITH GEMINI WOMAN

In love: Once their boundaries are clearly defined so there's no room for any misunderstanding, the Pisces man will mystify his Gemini lady as much as she will bamboozle him. A bizarre fascination can grow between these two as they sense that in this relationship they have found someone who understands their need for fluidity and spontaneity. It doesn't seem to matter much that they express that need in completely different ways. The Pisces man feels his way through life and while he appears to be confused, he's really just waiting for the right moment to move closer to his Gemini woman—or to swim away. Her fluidity is the result of her never-ending stream of thought about whether or not she fancies being with him. Sometimes she does and sometimes she doesn't. He'll commit sooner than she will, but one of his problems is his keenness to bare his soul to her too soon. This appeals to the Gemini lady and she could get hooked, but they should both try to assess the reality of the relationship before immersing themselves fully. They're both very changeable, but once they've decided to align themselves, they will have put together an apparently ideal partnership. Keeping up appearances may be a little more of a challenge, since there will be times when both will be blowing about at sea and will long for the other to provide directions or a safe harbor. That's when they could lose each other and simply drift out of each other's reach and they'll never be completely sure how they got swept so far apart.

 In bed: If, with her twin-cam, speedboat mind the Gemini girl can fathom the depths of the Fish and doesn't confuse him too much in the process, together they could create the ideal fantasy of man, woman, and more! These two are highly attracted to each other sexually and know instinctively that they could steam up a bedroom together. And they will, at least once, because they are equally and powerfully drawn by the other's enchanting sex appeal. However, when the experience is over, neither should be too surprised if the other has slipped away. The Pisces man is pursuing an emotional as well as a physical connection with a lover. He wants to feel her pleasure and won't be satisfied with her simply telling him what a good time she's having. And her constant sexy banter may even distract him and put him off his stroke, especially if there's the slightest hint of insincerity. He himself is unlikely to be honest about what bugs him.

The Gemini woman, on the other hand, needs to know that not just his body is engaged in their coming together. His silence could unnerve her; all she needs is some assurance or even just a squeak of approval. This liaison will kick-start itself, but uncertainty on both sides could lead to it fizzling rather than sizzling.

PISCES MAN WITH CANCER WOMAN

In love: Put two Water signs together—particularly the Pisces man and the Cancer woman—and what will the result be? A sublime sea of love and emotion. Words can't describe the depth of their mutual affection and understanding; they are almost telepathic in their ability to understand each other's needs and desires. In fact, they'll probably find that if they ever do need to talk, they'll end up doing so in sync. Once they become an item, they'll be finishing each other's sentences then giggling at themselves. To some extent, they'll love each other more as a couple than as individuals. Both are highly sensitive and appreciate the other's qualities equally. She makes him feel like a playful, happy child one minute, then inspires him to want to take care of her and spoil her the next. He can actually be what she wants him to be by being himself! He loves it that she admires his all-encompassing perspective on life and he delights in sharing his view with her. Together, the Pisces man and Cancer woman can make a magical, mystical world that only the two of them share—a place where they can let their imaginations flow. But the result won't simply be romantic nonsense that serves no purpose other than to fuel the intoxication of their hearts. They'll probably also be sowing the seeds of a more artistic and successful way of life together. These two are capable of inspiring one another to achieve more both spiritually and materially than either could achieve on their own.

 In bed: The Cancer woman and the Pisces man in bed are what erotic novels are made of. Their lovemaking reaches heights of ecstasy and passion that she never dreamed possible. He'll see only her elemental feminine beauty so she won't need to worry about the odd zit appearing on her face, while she's his ultimate fantasy woman, tender, responsive, and embracing. If she's a little reticent at times and presents a tough, impenetrable wall when he's busy pursuing her, he'll gently change course and find a way to dissolve her defenses until she reveals her soft, sweet center. He may sometimes seem to drift off into a world of his own while making love to her, but her imagination is as powerful as his, so there's no reason why she can't drift off with him. All this love, romance, and fantasy may sound wet and wimpish, but this is really more to do with what is going on in their hearts. When it comes to animal passion and erotic pleasure, there will be nothing wimpish about the Cancer woman and Pisces man. Their relationship is about idealism made real. It just gets better and better as time goes on.

PISCES MAN WITH **LEO WOMAN**

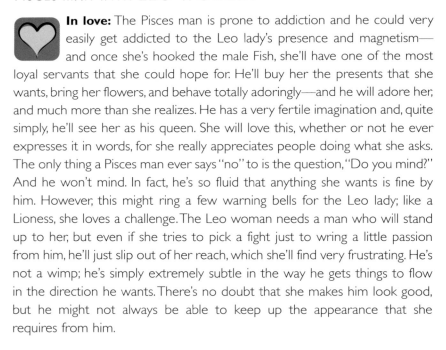

In love: The Pisces man is prone to addiction and he could very easily get addicted to the Leo lady's presence and magnetism—and once she's hooked the male Fish, she'll have one of the most loyal servants that she could hope for. He'll buy her the presents that she wants, bring her flowers, and behave totally adoringly—and he will adore her, and much more than she realizes. He has a very fertile imagination and, quite simply, he'll see her as his queen. She will love this, whether or not he ever expresses it in words, for she really appreciates people doing what she asks. The only thing a Pisces man ever says "no" to is the question, "Do you mind?" And he won't mind. In fact, he's so fluid that anything she wants is fine by him. However, this might ring a few warning bells for the Leo lady; like a Lioness, she loves a challenge. The Leo woman needs a man who will stand up to her, but even if she tries to pick a fight just to wring a little passion from him, he'll just slip out of her reach, which she'll find very frustrating. He's not a wimp; he's simply extremely subtle in the way he gets things to flow in the direction he wants. There's no doubt that she makes him look good, but he might not always be able to keep up the appearance that she requires from him.

In bed: The Pisces man will use his boundless imagination to set a scene where anything at all is possible. The Leo lady will do her best for him, too, which is more than enough. She's pretty creative herself and he'll gratefully lap up whatever she offers. With love as their aphrodisiac and their hearts locked together as well as their bodies, this can be an incredibly erotic experience for them both. The Pisces man simply doesn't know when to stop: he's oh so sensual that she'll soon be throbbing with anticipation, which is just the type of response that brings out the shark in the normally placid Mr. Fish. The Leo lady is quite creative, and her Pisces man will never run short of ideas to maintain the element of surprise and spontaneity in their sex life. When sex is the bait he becomes a single-minded predator. He will flow over his Leo lady's body like a deeply massaging waterfall and he will often leave her breathless. It often seems as if he's got an eternity to spend with her, which is wonderful, but she has other things to be getting on with and she may have to slip away at times to look after her kingdom.

PISCES MAN WITH VIRGO WOMAN

In love: The Virgo woman and Pisces man are totally in sympathy with one another; in some ways they are like two peas in a pod. They have a peculiar sensitivity to each other, but while she's able to put it into words, he feels it intuitively. He has a unique talent for getting around her inhibitions without her even noticing; he simply seeps into her consciousness and soothes away all her nerves. He makes it so easy for her to express herself, and can help her to discover and enter her hidden depths and passions. She does as much for him by providing an anchor for his imaginative wanderings. No longer will his musings remain a dream; she can show him how to turn them into reality. Her ability to see things clearly helps to lift the fog from his eyes and she's so willing to offer practical assistance that he feels that, with her by his side, he could go anywhere and do anything. Before they know it, this couple will be in love. The years will fly by, they'll have many good times together, and soon they'll be a happy old couple enjoying the same feelings of mutual love and wonder that they experienced when they met fifty years before!

 In bed: Since she's rather self-contained and a little nervous, it takes a special lover to make the Virgo woman really relax and let go, but if she wants to take the plunge and jump right in with the Fish, then he'll take her on a magical journey of sensual joy and beauty. It genuinely pleases him to please her so he's totally willing to bring her to an ecstatic high. He'll want to nibble and taste every part of this woman, and she'll have no choice but to succumb to his gentle yet voracious desires. Being with him will be a movingly emotional and spiritual experience, while he'll be so overwhelmed by her rapturous response to his touch that she'll have to fight for her turn to lavish her attentions on him. He needs to feel her physical presence and pleasure as much as she needs to feel his; it completes him and enraptures her. They'll learn a lot from each other about the art of lovemaking. He will school her in the delights of total surrender to the sensual experience and she'll show him how skillful touches, cleverly controlled, could rock his world and send him crashing into a new dimension of reality.

PISCES MAN WITH **LIBRA WOMAN**

In love: These two share a dreamy kind of love and are captivated by a sense of romance and mystery. At last they've found an idealist like themselves, someone who longs for the same merging of mind and soul, all of which adds to the element of perfection in their relationship; they reach the point where they are completely at peace and in love with one another. The Pisces man will have the Libra lady believing his tales of make-believe so that they'll soon be imagining themselves floating on heavenly clouds, wrapped in gossamer-light robes, and listening to beautiful, other-worldly music. But hang on! Back on earth, in the real world, things aren't quite as magical as that! At times, Lady Libra could find herself walking on eggshells around this very sensitive man, especially when she pulls him up on one of his many unkept promises, and that can get a little draining for both of them. He means well, it's just that the fantasy feels better than the reality. While he wants to express their connection in an emotional manner, that's a bit too wishy-washy for her. Her preference is for an accord based on verbally expressed ideas, but no matter how flowery the language, he finds that too dry. He might feel under pressure in a relationship with the Libra lady and may end up floating off on one of those fluffy clouds all on his own. He shouldn't be surprised, though, when he looks back, to see her fanning the wind to help speed his departure.

In bed: The Pisces man can whip up a real-life fantasy in bed faster than Aunt Jemima can whip up a round of pancakes. All the Libra lady needs to do is to tell him one of her sexy stories and he'll catch her drift and turn it into a fast-moving current of sexual passion. That's when the Pisces man comes alive. He's so seductive and what's so sweet is that he doesn't seem at all sure of himself. He'll make love to her and make her feel loved like she's never been loved before and he'll immerse himself totally in her romantic fantasies, then turn them up a notch on the sex-o-meter. But there's one small catch—she shouldn't expect to be allowed up for air! He'll be in for the duration and she'll know it. He truly wants to lose himself in her, with no holds barred and no time limit. But if the Libra lady doesn't respond in the totally involved way that the shy Pisces man needs her to, then he'll probably droop over her like a wet blanket. This is such a shame for both of them because nothing turns a Libra lady off faster than feeling the weight of emotion bearing down on her when all she wants is to be lifted to the heights of erotic bliss. She's an enigma and it's not easy for him to get a real grip on her.

PISCES MAN WITH **SCORPIO WOMAN**

In love: There may never be a better combination of ethereal lovers than the Scorpio woman and Pisces man. She feels him coming her way before she even sets eyes on him because everything happens on an instinctive and intuitive level between these two.

The Pisces man is the most willing target in the zodiac for the irresistibly alluring Scorpio woman's seduction. He wants to fall right into her and lose himself there completely. She feels totally herself plus a little bit more when she's in his company, and when they're together, neither needs anybody else. The spiritual and emotional bond between them is potent; the mental and physical connection is complete. However, there's always a catch when fishing for Pisces: Scorpio is possessive and uses a pincer-like hold, but elusive Pisces can slip off any hook if he feels caught. As long as they both recognize how loyal they are and can give each other a lot of slack, they make the almost ideal couple. They're both sensitive and loving, and both feel more secure, creative, and playful as a double act than when they're going solo. The estimated duration of this relationship is from now until kingdom come. Even if, for some bizarre reason, they end up at each other's throats, neither the love between them nor the memory of it will ever die. There's an element of destiny about their being together, so if this magical couple don't manage to work it out in this lifetime, they'll do so the next time around.

 In bed: In a word—intoxicating! Getting dreamily drunk on love and addicted to the effects of this highly emotional coupling is only to be expected. If they're looking for an out-of-body experience, then the Scorpio woman will find sex with a Pisces man is about the closest thing to it, and vice versa. When these two Water signs get down to it, they go deep, deep down. There are no limits to the depths of their closeness or to the heights to which their spirits soar when the passionate

Scorpio woman meets up with the ultimately romantic Pisces man. This is mutual worship at its very best. He'll sacrifice himself to her sexual pleasure but will gain the world in return, and she'll keep for him exclusively the erotic intensity of her sweet, sensitive heart. It will be as though she were wearing an invisible chastity belt that only his love key can open. These two are inclined to lose all concept of time and space when they're together; even a short moment of afternoon delight could end up in a seriously expanded time warp. On occasions like that it would be wise to check the calendar rather than the clock.

PISCES MAN WITH **SAGITTARIUS WOMAN**

In love: There's an unreal quality to the attraction between the Pisces man and the Sagittarius woman. They both have their own individual way of looking at life as if through a magnifying glass. One of them will be examining what they say, the other what they do, but whichever area of their life is under the microscope, it will have an alluring and hypnotic appeal. It can also be completely infuriating! One thing is sure, though; they won't fail to fascinate and flow around one another. When they actually connect and enter the physical realm, however, it might feel as though something doesn't quite live up to its promise. Then they'll try again and again, dancing a strange dance that never ends or, in some cases, never truly satisfies. This could spiral upward into a heavenly waltz that inspires them and gives them something to aspire to, or it may go in the opposite direction and feel like a hellish jive on broken glass. They both encourage the other's pursuits, but because they jump to their own conclusions as to what's really going on, they may simply encourage each other in completely the wrong direction. That's when they could start blaming each other for their own mistakes; she'll ride roughshod over his sensitivity and he'll refuse to be hooked by responsibility. When this relationship is good, it feels as if there's not only a heart, mind, and body connection, but an irresistible spiritual bond as well. But when it's not so good, it might be better if the romantic Mr. Fish swam away and the Lady Archer aimed her arrows of love at another target.

 In bed: There's no doubt about it, this is a sexy, steamy, saucy, sweet, and extremely sensual entanglement. It will be whatever they both dream it to be. Both have vast imaginations that are capable of making even the most ordinary situation into a real-life fairytale. They'll immerse themselves in the moment and get fired up and carried away on a fantastical journey, only to return to reality with nothing to show for their journey and not at all sure where they've been. The Pisces man is after an emotional link when he indulges in the pleasures of the flesh, and he'll strive to find and maintain one, but Lady Sagittarius simply doesn't have the emotional staying power he needs. She may not be able to provide the soft, lovey-dovey doe-eyed looks that really limber up his libido and satisfy his longing. Instead, she'll offer him a well of ecstasy to dive into and lose himself in, but while he's in there swimming around and looking to bring back that loving feeling, she'll be off on a wild sexual tangent, leaving him a little at a loss as to how to catch her. That's when it wouldn't be a good idea for him to flop about like a fish out of water just because things aren't perfect. A Sagittarius lady needs a firm sense of direction and won't be happy if she's left to travel the path to erotic bliss all on her own.

PISCES MAN WITH **CAPRICORN WOMAN**

 In love: The Capricorn woman will really fall for the dreamy, romantic Pisces guy. She's a closet romantic herself, and he nudges her in just the right way to bring it all tumbling out into the open. He encourages her to share her feelings with him and talk about emotional issues, which is something she finds quite unique in a man. In return, she will listen to him when he wants to say how he feels, for she can easily contain the vast well of emotion that he has to express. His imagination and sensitivity capture her heart, providing her with a much-needed sense of relaxation while still giving the feeling of purpose that will build a close and loving bond between them. He is easily addicted to her expressive sensuality and is very impressed by her wisdom and the hard-earned symbols of her success. Both of them have such lofty ideals and such breadth of understanding that it's fantastic for them to have found someone with whom they can share their thoughts. They could get so wound up in each other, however, that other important people and tasks in their lives get left behind, which, in the long run, will freak out the Capricorn woman and not be healthy for the Pisces man. Their love does have such potential for development that it will keep them both happy for many years. It could surely be the most beautiful and romantic relationship the Capricorn woman will ever have, and the most deeply secure, supportive, and profound relationship of the Pisces man.

 In bed: For all his shyness and sensitivity, Mr. Pisces is more than a match for the insatiable physical appetites of Ms. Capricorn. There's a sense of relief when these two come together and release their tension. Although, in their own way, both can be shy, when they get together they are eager to reveal themselves to one another, for there's an unspoken feeling of love and acceptance between them. Their inhibitions are stripped away as they remove each item of clothing. He wants to show himself in his full glory and lose himself completely in her, and she'll be keen and very welcoming. She might be very much in control of herself with other lovers, but this guy makes it possible for her to truly surrender and be carried away on waves of passion. If she's hooked on this Fish, she definitely won't want to throw him back, and once he's seen who's caught him, he won't let her! The Capricorn woman has exactly what this Pisces man has been looking for in a lover—an intense sensuality that rocks the very foundations of his desire. Her sexuality is solid and secure but if there are any cracks, he'll find them and fill them with his own brand of sensuality so that they both feel complete.

PISCES MAN WITH AQUARIUS WOMAN

In love: The Pisces man will fascinate the Aquarius woman in the most hypnotic way and she will appeal to his desire for something beyond the here and now. Unlike many women, she understands the Pisces man, that is until he begins to talk about emotions. He'll have to trust his instincts when it comes to her emotional commitment because she may sound a little dry and analytical whenever he attempts to immerse her in conversation about it. She'll simply switch off or go off on a different intellectual tangent but, luckily, he'll just start thinking about whatever it is she's talking about. He's intuitive and empathetic, so he's capable of following her intellectual lead. He'll blend into her and she'll encourage his individuality, so they can be very good for one another. These two will be so impressed with each other on a mental and a spiritual level, that it may take the Aquarius woman a long time to realize that, beneath the surface, her Pisces lover is a very sensitive man. Similarly, he won't initially recognize her need for independence. By this point they may already be in love—which amounts to commitment—though she may find it difficult to verbalize it. She may be too detached for him; his insecurities need a lot of emotional support, and this doesn't come naturally to the Aquarius girl. However, with a little work and a lot of love, these two could end up as a very heavenly match.

In bed: For this couple, sex will rarely start in bed. It's more likely to begin when they're out doing something else, like the grocery shopping, and if they find any opportunities for double entendres, then the jokes will start. They'll carry on all the way home until, as they come through the door, they can hardly keep their hands off one another. When Lady Aquarius finally slides into bed with her horny Pisces man, she'll realize that this is an experience that will take her over the edge and beyond. And he won't stop at the usual boundaries of erotic togetherness so she could find herself floating off into a fantasy land, where she loses touch with her body and with what's happening on the physical plane. He knows instinctively that she's a lover who's capable of stratospheric levels of pleasure and he knows how to release her inner sex goddess. That all sounds very lovely, but then she comes down to earth with a bump. Never mind. There's definitely more to this couple than just being in bed together. They're making love all the time, whether it's with sassy, saucy suggestions over the phone, or by making dirty bedroom eyes at one another across the table at a dinner party. The best thing is that they always live up to their promises and take those promises all the way.

PISCES MAN WITH **PISCES WOMAN**

See pages 72–74.